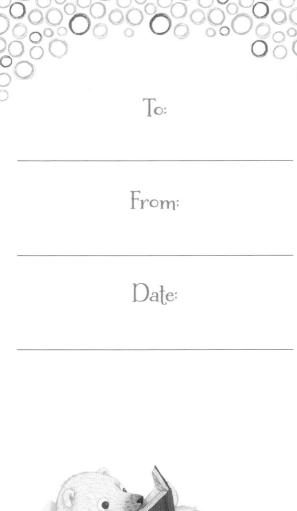

To:

_____

From:

_____

Date:

_____

100
Favorite
Bible Verses
for Children

ILLUSTRATED BY

MIRIAM LATIMER &
JULIANNE ST. CLAIR

A Division of Thomas Nelson Publishers

100 Favorite Bible Verses for Children
© 2017 by Thomas Nelson

Published in Nashville, Tennessee, by Tommy Nelson. Tommy Nelson is an imprint of Thomas Nelson. Thomas Nelson is a registered trademark of HarperCollins Christian Publishing, Inc.

Illustrated by Miriam Latimer and Julianne St. Clair

Tommy Nelson titles may be purchased in bulk for educational, business, fund-raising, or sales promotional use. For information, please e-mail SpecialMarkets@ThomasNelson.com.

ISBN-13: 978-0-7180-9945-9

Library of Congress Cataloging-in-Publication Data

Names: Fischer, Jean, 1952- author. | Latimer, Miriam, illustrator.
Title: 100 favorite Bible verses for children / Jean Fischer; illustrated by Miriam Latimer
Other titles: One hundred favorite Bible verses for children
Description: Nashville : Thomas Nelson, 2017.
Identifiers: LCCN 2017000438 | ISBN 9780718099459 (hardcover)
Subjects: LCSH: Children—Prayers and devotions. | Bibl—Quotations.
Classification: LCC BV4870 .F57 2017 | DDC 220.5/208—dc23 LC record available at https://lccn.loc.gov/2017000438

Printed in China

17 18 19 20 21 DSC 6 5 4 3 2 1

Mfr: DSC / Shenzhen, China / October 2017 / PO #9452773

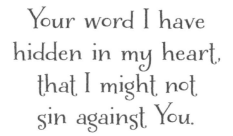

Your word I have
hidden in my heart,
that I might not
sin against You.

—Psalm 119:11 NKJV

A Letter to Parents

W hat is your favorite verse in the Bible?
Maybe a certain verse impacted you as a
child, and you've held it close ever since. Or maybe you haven't been able to narrow your favorites
down to just one—there are too many precious
verses to choose from!

These cherished verses are a powerful force in
our lives. They give us strength when we are weak,
encourage us when we are down, and remind us of
God's love and His plan for us whenever we lose
our way. God's Word speaks to each person, from
the oldest to the youngest, and it's never too early
to start learning the Bible!

Helping children discover the Bible is an exciting part of parenting. Take a few moments to sit
with your child and introduce some of the most-

loved verses in the Bible—perhaps for the very first time! Reading the fun and sweet devotions will help young children understand what the verses mean and how to apply them in their own lives. As you read, you will become closer to each other as you both draw closer to God.

This book can also be used as a tool to memorize Scripture. The verses we hide in our hearts will stay with us, guiding and encouraging us for all of our lives. So snuggle up with your child and *100 Favorite Bible Verses for Children*, and discover His Word together.

1

....

God's Kind of Love

God loves you, and He wants you to love others too—with His kind of love.

Read 1 Corinthians 13:4–5. While you read it, replace the words *love* and *it* with your own name.

Now you know how God wants you to love others!

Ask God who He wants you to love today. He may remind you of someone you need to forgive (because "love does not remember wrongs"). He may want you to pray about waiting (because "love is patient"), or God may lead you to make a card for someone who is sick or to help around the house without being asked (because love is "kind"). Listen for God's direction, and then do whatever He says. A good feeling comes into your heart when you obey God and love others with His kind of love.

God, teach me to love with
Your kind of love.

1 Corinthians 13:4–5 ICB

Love is patient and kind. Love is not jealous, it does not brag, and it is not proud. Love is not rude, is not selfish, and does not become angry easily. Love does not remember wrongs done against it.

2

Don't Be Afraid

Look around. Who do you see? Do you see your mom or dad? Maybe your sister or brother is nearby. Maybe you only see your favorite pet. But someone else is with you too. Do you know who it is?

It's God!

God is always with you—at home, at school, at a friend's house. He's everywhere! God goes wherever you go. He sees everything you do. Nothing that happens surprises God because He knows everything.

Sometimes you might feel worried or afraid. God understands. That's why He wants you to remember that He is with you wherever you go. When you're scared, remember that God says, "Be strong and brave. . . . Don't be afraid." Whatever happens, God is beside you and won't ever leave you. You can always count on Him to help you.

Thank You, God, for always being with me, wherever I go.

Joshua 1:9 ICB

"Remember that I commanded
you to be strong and brave.
So don't be afraid. The Lord
your God will be with you
everywhere you go."

3

The Good Shepherd

A shepherd is someone who takes care of sheep. A shepherd makes sure the sheep are safe from harm and have food, water, and a place to rest.

Did you know that Jesus is like a shepherd? He is sometimes called the Good Shepherd.

And people can be like sheep. We gather in crowds. Sometimes we're afraid and unsure of what to do. We can be stubborn, and we don't always obey. That's why we need the Good Shepherd to lead us.

Jesus watches over His people just as a shepherd watches over his sheep. There is nothing that Jesus won't do for us. He makes sure we have everything we need. If we are lost, Jesus finds us. When we feel afraid, He comforts us. Jesus never leaves His people. He is with us all day and all night!

Jesus, with You as the Good Shepherd, I have everything I need.

Psalm 23:1-3 NCV

The LORD is my shepherd;
I have everything I need.
He lets me rest in green pastures.
He leads me to calm water.
He gives me new strength.

4

God Forgives Me

Everyone sins—you, your friends, your parents, and even people you read about in the Bible. The only person who hasn't done anything wrong is Jesus.

And when you disobey, nothing seems right. You feel worried and upset. Your tummy might even hurt or feel sick. That's what sin does to you. Sin takes away all your good feelings.

God does not want us to feel sick and upset forever. That's why He sent Jesus. When Jesus died on the cross, He saved us from sin. John, one of Jesus' friends, said that if we tell God when we do something wrong, He will forgive us. God washes away all those bad feelings that sin brings. His forgiveness makes us feel good and clean inside as if that sin never happened.

Dear God, I'm sorry for the wrong things I've done. Please forgive me.

1 John 1:9 ICB

If we confess our sins, he will
forgive our sins. We can trust
God. He does what is right.
He will make us clean from
all the wrongs we have done.

5

Be Like Jesus

How do you make a peanut butter sandwich? First, you open the bag of bread and take out two pieces. Next, you unscrew the lid on the peanut butter jar. Using a knife, you spread some peanut butter on one piece of the bread. Then you put the other piece of bread on top, and you're done! Can you imagine making this sandwich? It would be a lot easier if someone showed you how to make it.

Showing someone how to do something is often better than telling. God knows that, so He sent us Jesus. God wants us to live the way Jesus did: to do what is right, to love being kind, to trust God, and to never think we are better than anyone else. Jesus always obeyed God. He did what God wanted Him to do even if He didn't feel like doing it.

Remember how Jesus lived, and do your best to be like Him.

Jesus, please show me how
I can be more like You.

Micah 6:8 ICB

The Lord has told you what is good. He has told you what he wants from you: Do what is right to other people. Love being kind to others. And live humbly, trusting your God.

6

Love God and Others!

A man asked Jesus, "What does someone need to do to live forever in heaven?"

Jesus said you have to love God more than anything and love others as much as you love yourself.

You can show love to God by reading the Bible, spending time talking with Him, and obeying what He says to do. When you love God more than anything else, He fills you up with His love. You have so much love inside that it spills over. And His love helps you know how special you are. It's easy to love who you are when you remember how much God loves you.

But God doesn't want you to keep this love to yourself. He wants you to share it! You can love others by being friendly and helping them, the way Jesus did.

Dear God, help me to love
You more each day and to
love myself and others.

Luke 10:27 NKJV

"'You shall love the LORD your God with all your heart, with all your soul, with all your strength,  and with all your mind,' and 'your neighbor as yourself.'"

7

Jesus Made a Way!

God loved everyone in the world so much that He sent His only Son, Jesus, to do something very special. Jesus made a way for everyone to live in heaven someday!

Everybody has sinned, which means we've all disobeyed God. The punishment for sinning is being separated from God. But God didn't want that, so He allowed Jesus to be punished for everyone's sins. Jesus gave up His own life. He hung on a cross and died, and then all the people who believed in Jesus were forgiven for the wrong things they did.

But then something else happened. God made Jesus come alive again! God promised that anyone who believes that Jesus died for their sins and came alive again will live forever in heaven with God someday. Isn't that a wonderful promise?

Thank You, God, for Jesus!

John 3:16 ICB

"For God loved the world so much that he gave his only Son. God gave his Son so that whoever believes in him may not be lost, but have eternal life."

8

Ruth Follows God

The Bible tells the story of Ruth and Naomi. Ruth was a young woman, and Naomi was old. It was not good for Naomi to be alone, so Ruth promised never to leave her. Ruth gave up her home and being near her family to go live with Naomi. It was hard for Ruth to be away from home. But she chose to follow what God wanted her to do, to live with Naomi.

When you have a hard choice to make, say a prayer and ask God to help you. Trust Him to show you what is right. Then be brave and get going! Follow God. Trust Him to be with you and to lead the way.

Thank You, God, for being my best friend. I love You. I will be Your friend forever.

Ruth 1:16 ICB

Don't ask me to leave you!
Don't beg me not to follow you!
Every place you go, I will go.
Every place you live, I will live.
Your people will be my people.
Your God will be my God.

9

God Shows Me the Way

What if your family went on a trip, but no one knew how to get to where you were going? The map on your smart phone would help. But the best thing to do is to get directions before you ever leave.

The same is true about your everyday life. Have you ever been unsure of what you should do or say? To do the right thing, you have to listen to directions and follow them.

God is the best at giving directions. He wants to teach you how to live in ways that please Him. When you read the Bible, pray, and listen for His voice in your heart, God will show you what He wants you to do. Then when you follow His directions , you will become wise.

God, please show me what I should do. Help me to listen and follow Your directions.

Psalm 32:8 NCV

The LORD says, "I will make you wise and show you where to go. I will guide you and watch over you."

10

Pray All the Time

Prayer is talking with God. When you talk with Him, you are talking with the Creator of the universe, the one and only God. Wow! That's amazing, isn't it? Our great big God cares about what we have to say.

Do you ever pray to God? It's easy to do! Just tell Him whatever is on your mind. You can ask Him to help you when you have to do something hard, and you can thank Him for all the wonderful things He has given you. You can tell Him about your day, and He will understand because He was with you the whole time.

Remember this: God is always with you. Whenever you feel worried, God is there. Talk with Him. Ask Him to calm you down. Then God will replace all those worries with His peace.

God, thank You for hearing all my prayers.

Philippians 4:6 ICB

Do not worry about anything.
But pray and ask God for
everything you need. And when
you pray, always give thanks.

11

Like an Eagle

Have you ever seen an eagle? Eagles are big, strong birds. They fly fast and dive even faster. They can soar a half mile above the earth! If you've ever seen an eagle, then you know how powerful they are.

Isaiah 40:31 promises that God will make you strong—strong like an eagle. Everyone feels down sometimes, even kids! When you feel unhappy or tired, pray and ask God to help. God never gets tired. He is always ready to take care of you, so you can trust that He will lift you up. Then imagine that you are flying high above earth, happy and carefree, just like an eagle.

> Dear God, when I feel tired
> or unhappy, I will trust You
> to help me feel better.

Isaiah 40:31 ICB

The people who trust the Lord will become strong again. They will be able to rise up as an eagle in the sky. They will run without needing rest. They will walk without becoming tired.

12

A Hurt That Helps

Some things that hurt can be good for you. Think about shots. They don't feel good, but that little pinch protects you from the flu. If you scrape your knee, Mom puts medicine on it that stings a little. But the medicine helps heal the scrape.

God's words in the Bible can hurt sometimes too. We feel bad when God's words remind us that we have disobeyed Him.

Think about how you felt after you did something wrong. You wanted to feel better about it, didn't you? Hebrews 4:12 says that when God's words remind you of a wrong thing you did, it's like being poked gently with a sword. But this reminder is good! It teaches us to run to God for forgiveness.

God will always forgive you. He will take away the hurt and help you do better next time.

God, I'm sorry for disobeying You. Thank You for reminding me that I should do better.

Hebrews 4:12 ICB

God's word is alive and working. It is sharper than a sword sharpened on both sides. It cuts all the way into us, where the soul and the spirit are joined. It cuts to the center of our joints and our bones. And God's word judges the thoughts and feelings in our hearts.

13

God Can Do Anything!

Jesus fed a crowd of people with one boy's simple lunch. Jesus took the boy's five small loaves of bread and two little fish, and He turned them into enough to feed more than five thousand people! The Bible is filled with stories about God making impossible things happen. Nothing is impossible for God. He can do anything!

Is there something that you find impossible to do? Ask God to help you. Do you know other people who need God's help? Ask God to help them too. Even when something seems impossible, we can have hope— because everything is possible with God!

Dear God, help me to trust that everything is possible with You.

Luke 1:37 NKJV

For with God nothing
will be impossible.

14

God's Treasure Chest

Think about all your stuff—your toys, the things in your room, the stuff in your backpack, your clothes. If you had a treasure chest, what one favorite thing would you put inside it?

God's treasure chest is different than a chest filled with stuff. His holds things like kindness toward others, helpfulness, forgiveness, joy, and love. Those things are most important to God.

Did you know you have a treasure chest in heaven? When you are kind, helpful, forgiving, happy, and loving, it is like putting those things in your treasure chest there. Heaven is the safest place they can be. Someday when you get to heaven, you can open your treasure chest and see all the things you have put inside.

Dear God, help me treasure
what is important to You.

Matthew 6:20-21 ICB

"Store your treasure in heaven.
The treasures in heaven cannot
be destroyed by moths or rust.
And thieves cannot break in and
steal that treasure. Your heart
will be where your treasure is."

15

Something from Nothing

In the beginning, before the earth or sky or anything else existed, there was only God. Everything was dark. So God said, "Let there be light!" And the darkness went away. God made it happen. It was easy! God is so great that He can create things just by wanting them to be there.

When you draw a picture, you need paper and crayons. When you bake cupcakes, you need ingredients like flour and sugar. But when God makes things, He doesn't need anything. God just says the words and it happens.

God made the earth, the oceans, and the mountains from nothing. He made animals and people just by wanting them to exist. God is that powerful! Nothing is impossible for Him—nothing at all.

God, You are so great.
You can do anything!

Genesis 1:3 NIV

God said, "Let there be light," and there was light.

16

....

A Big Hug

Imagine a shepherd caring for his sheep. He hears a little lamb crying. He sees that it is afraid. So the shepherd picks up the lamb and hugs it close.

You know how that lamb feels. When you are sad or afraid, there is nothing better than a hug. You feel someone's strong arms wrap around you. They hold you close. You feel loved, and you know that everything will be all right.

Jesus is like that shepherd. He hears you when you cry. He knows when you are afraid. Jesus wants to pick you up and hold you in His arms. So, whenever you feel sad or afraid, think about Jesus holding you close, giving you the biggest, warmest hug ever! Then you can be sure that everything will be all right.

Jesus, I need You. Help
me to feel Your warm hug
when I'm sad or afraid.

Isaiah 40:11 ICB

The Lord takes care of his
people like a shepherd. He
gathers the people like lambs
in his arms. He carries them
close to him. He gently leads
the mothers of the lambs.

17

God Is So Good!

Can you name some good things God has done for you? He gave you a place to live, food to eat, friends, and family. The best thing God gave us is His Son, Jesus, and we can live with Him in heaven someday. God is so good!

Think about a time when things did not go your way. You felt sad or angry, but then you asked God for help. And after a while things got better. That's because when you trust God, He will always help you. He turns your frowns to smiles. He dries your tears and makes you happy again.

Remember this: God is good all the time. In every kind of trouble you can always trust Him to help.

Dear God, You are so good to me! Thank You for helping me.

Psalm 118:5 NCV

I was in trouble, so I called to
the LORD. The LORD answered
me and set me free.

18

"Father God, Hear My Prayers."

God loves you, and He loves hearing your voice. He wants you to talk with Him all the time. God has the power to do whatever you ask of Him, but when you pray, He wants you to pray with faith. Praying with faith means you believe that God hears you and will answer your prayers.

God might not answer your prayers right away. But He always hears you. He might not give you what you want. But He always knows what is best for you. He knows exactly what you need and when you need it. When you believe in God and keep praying to Him, He makes great things happen.

Remember, your heavenly Father is your best friend. Talk with Him because you love Him. Trust Him to do great things for you.

Father God, help me trust You to answer my prayers.

James 5:16 NCV

When a believing person
prays, great things happen.

19

Paul

The apostle Paul knew all about feeling weak. He kept asking God to take away his problems. But God said, "My grace is enough for you."

Paul couldn't fix his troubles alone. He needed God's help. But when God didn't help right away, Paul did not stop praying. He kept trusting God. The more Paul trusted, the stronger His trust got! Paul believed with his whole heart that God could fix his problems. But when God did not fix them, Paul still felt happy. He believed God was good and that God loved him. Paul knew God would do what was best for him at just the right time. Even if he had to wait.

Dear God, when You don't answer my prayers right away, please make me strong by trusting in You.

2 Corinthians 12:9–10 ICB

The Lord said to me, "My grace is enough for you. When you are weak, then my power is made perfect in you." So I am very happy to brag about my weaknesses. Then Christ's power can live in me. So I am happy when I have weaknesses, insults, hard times, sufferings, and all kinds of troubles. All these things are for Christ. And I am happy, because when I am weak, then I am truly strong.

20

If I Belong to Jesus

After reading Romans 8:1, you might think, *The Bible says no one can punish me because I belong to Jesus, so I can disobey and get away with it!*

That's not what this Bible verse means. When you disobey, you deserve a time-out or whatever else your parents decide is best. It is their job to help you learn to do what is right. But Romans 8:1 is talking about the biggest punishment of all—being separated from God forever.

God didn't want that punishment for you or anyone else. So He sent Jesus. If you believe Jesus died on the cross for your sins, then you belong to Jesus forever. When you belong to Jesus, God promises to forgive you any time you disobey. And He gave another wonderful promise—You get to live with Him someday!

Thank You, God, for sending
Jesus so I can live with You
in heaven someday.

Romans 8:1 CEV

If you belong to Christ Jesus,
you won't be punished.

21

Shhh...Let's Be Quiet

You can talk with God wherever you are. He is with you even in the loudest places: at a parade with trumpets trumpeting and drums booming, or in a storm with whooshing wind and crashing thunder. Wherever you are, you can talk with God, and He hears you.

But God knows that your best talks happen when you are quiet and still. That's why it is important to find a quiet place every day to spend time with God. In the quiet, you can feel nearest to Him. You can tell Him whatever is on your mind. Or you can just sit still and feel Him close to you.

Go to your quiet place today. Have a talk with God.

Here I am, God, quiet
and still. Let's talk!

Psalm 46:10 NIV

"Be still, and know
that I am God."

22

·············

The Spirit of God

Paul wanted his friends to know about God's power and the great things God can do. So Paul wrote them a letter about God's Spirit. Ephesians 1:17 is part of the letter he wrote.

Did you know that God does not have a body like humans do? You can't see God. But you can feel His Spirit all around you and also in your heart. It is that feeling that makes you want to know more about God. It's also that great feeling you get when you remember God loves you. God's Spirit helps you to trust and teaches you important things.

Paul prayed and asked God's Spirit to come into His friends' hearts. You can pray and ask God for His Spirit too. Ask Him to come into your heart and into the hearts of your friends.

Dear God, please fill my heart
and the hearts of my friends with
Your great and powerful Spirit.

Ephesians 1:17 CEV

I ask the glorious Father and God of our Lord Jesus Christ to give you his Spirit. The Spirit will make you wise and let you understand what it means to know God.

23

......

A Safe Place to Hide

Big rocks are almost impossible to move. Sometimes it takes powerful machines to break a rock into smaller pieces so it can be carried away.

In the Bible, a king named David said that God is like a giant rock, but with one big difference—nothing can break Him. God is too mighty, powerful, and great to be broken. David said that God is more powerful than just one rock. God is more like a wall made of strong, hard rocks, a wall that nothing can get through. David knew that when he was worried or afraid, he had a safe place waiting for him: God's strong protection.

God will take care of you, just as He took care of David. Go to Him when you need to feel safe.

Dear God, You are strong, like
a big wall of rocks! I know I am
safe when I am with You.

Psalm 62:2 NIV

Truly he is my rock and my salvation; he is my fortress, I will never be shaken.

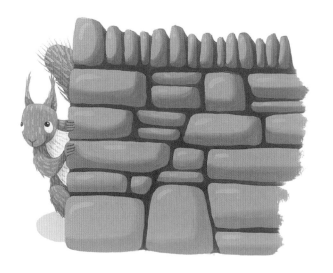

24

I Will Be Like Jesus

When Jesus lived on earth, He always did good things for others. Jesus was God's Son, but He never thought of Himself as being better than others. He helped people, healed them of sickness, and taught them the right way to live. Jesus gave up His own life so people could live in heaven one day.

Jesus wants you to do your best to live the way He did. Never think that you are better than anyone. Love others. Help them. Obey God. And show others the right way to live by setting a good example.

Remember that Jesus is your Lord and good friend. Kneel down and pray to Him. Ask Him to help you be more like Him.

Here I am, Lord Jesus. Teach me to love and help others like You did.

Philippians 2:5–6 ICB

In your lives you must think
and act like Christ Jesus.
Christ himself was like God in
everything. He was equal with
God. But he did not think
that being equal with God was
something to be held on to.

25

The Bible

The Bible is God's book written for us—His people. When we read the Bible, or someone reads it to us, we learn important lessons. We see how much God loves us. We discover the wonderful ways He helps us. And we find out how God wants us to live.

The Bible also tells about Jesus and how God sent Him to earth to make a way for us to get to heaven. It teaches us how to be more like Jesus. It tells us to share Jesus with our friends.

Whether you have your own Bible that you read or someone reads the Bible to you, try to listen to God's words. Think about them. Get in the habit of learning from the Bible every day.

Thank You, God, for the
Bible. I can't wait to hear all
that You have to tell me.

2 Timothy 3:16–17 CEV

Everything in the Scriptures is God's Word. All of it is useful for teaching and helping people and for correcting them and showing them how to live. The Scriptures train God's servants to do all kinds of good deeds.

26

I Make God Happy

What makes God happy? His people do—and that includes you!

God loves you. When you love Him back, He's joyful. God is even happier when He knows you love His Son, Jesus. God's happiness grows when you do your best to follow Jesus and live like He did. God fills up with joy when you tell others about Him. The Bible says that you make God in heaven so happy that He sings about you!

Always remember that you are God's child. Wherever you go, God is with you—at home, school, church, everywhere! You can count on Him for everything you need. And when you are sad, afraid, or tired, God quiets you with His love.

What can you do for God? You can make Him very happy by living a life that is right and good.

Dear God, help me to remember that you love me and are singing over me!

Zephaniah 3:17 NKJV

The LORD your God in your midst,
The Mighty One, will save; He will
rejoice over you with gladness,
He will quiet you with His love, He
will rejoice over you with singing.

27

Hooray for Today!

Today is a special day. Do you know why? Each day is special because God made it. Today is somebody's birthday. Today someone will win a race or get a perfect score in a game or on a test. Today is the day someone makes a new friend or enjoys time with an old one. Today people will love and help each other.

Your whole life is made up of days. They are God's gifts to you. Maybe God will surprise you today with something unexpected.

Look for one special thing that God does for you today. Then tell your family about it. Say a prayer together, and thank God for His gifts. Celebrate the wonderful things He does for you each day.

Lord, thank You for all my days.
What special things do You
have planned for me today?

Psalm 118:24 NKJV

This is the day the LORD has made; we will rejoice and be glad in it.

28

Jesus Understands

When you think of Jesus, do you think of a grown-up man? It's true that the Bible mostly tells us about Jesus as a grown-up. But Jesus was once a baby, like you were. He was a kid, like you are right now. Jesus learned to walk and talk, like you did. He helped His parents. And sometimes He felt sad or hurt. Jesus was a lot like you!

One thing about Jesus was different. He was perfect. He never disobeyed God. He was the only One who ever was or ever will be perfect. Still, He understands what it is like to be a kid and a grown-up. Jesus understands you!

Come to Jesus with all your problems. Don't be shy. He knows just how you feel, and Jesus will always help you.

Jesus, I'm so glad that you were a kid once. You understand what it's like to be me!

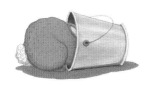

Hebrews 4:15–16 CEV

Jesus understands every weakness of ours, because he was tempted in every way that we are. But he did not sin! So whenever we are in need, we should come bravely before the throne of our merciful God. There we will be treated with undeserved kindness, and we will find help.

29

God Gives Peace

Today you had to wear the outfit your mom wanted you to put on, even though you didn't want to. Later you got a time-out for misbehaving. Then you fell at the playground and hurt your elbow. Everything is going wrong, and you're having a bad day.

Everyone has a bad day sometimes. It feels like a big rain cloud that follows you everywhere. Your heart is unhappy, and nothing in the world is right.

But don't worry! Your heavenly Father is bigger than the world! There isn't anything that surprises God about your day. He knows what's going on, and He's working out all your troubles. Whenever you have a not-so-good day, remember that God is there. He will calm you down and fill your heart with His peace.

Dear God, I need a peaceful
heart today. Will you calm me
down and help me, please?

John 16:33 NIV

"I have told you these things, so that in me you may have peace. In this world you will have trouble. But take heart! I have overcome the world."

61

30

···········

Work Hard

Do you think you would like to be more like someone else? Maybe you wish you were a better reader like your older brother. Or better at sports like your sister. It is good to want to do your best work all the time. But the Bible says that you shouldn't compare yourself with others. God gives each person different gifts and talents. He made each of us special.

Maybe you are good at singing or dancing. Maybe you are good at puzzles, drawing, or helping around the house. If you put the things you're good at together with someone else and what they're good at, you can do great things together!

Whatever you do well, work hard at it. This makes God happy. When you do your work well, you can be proud of what you have done.

Heavenly Father, thank
You for giving me my own
special gifts and talents.

Galatians 6:4-5 CEV

Do your own work well, and then you will have something to be proud of. But don't compare yourself with others. We each must carry our own load.

31

A Man Named Job

Blessings are those things God puts in your life that make you happy. Blessings can be little, like warm chocolate chip cookies. Or big, like getting a present that you wanted or making a new friend. Blessings help you remember how much God loves you. And they help you to love God even more.

But what if God let someone take all your blessings away? Would you still love Him?

That's what happened to a man named Job. God gave Job a test to show that he trusted God. God allowed all of Job's blessings to be taken. And Job passed God's test! He did not get angry with God. He kept on loving God and trusting Him—even when He had nothing. Then God blessed Job with even more than He had before.

Could you keep on trusting God if all of your blessings went away?

God, help me trust You no matter what happens.

Job 23:10 ICB

God knows the way that I
take. When he has tested me,
I will come out pure as gold.

32

Tell Others About Jesus

You are learning so much about Jesus. You know that He is God's Son and that He is good, kind, and perfect. Jesus does great things. He died so people can be forgiven for their sins and go to heaven. You know Jesus loves everyone. He teaches the right way to live, and best of all, Jesus is your friend and the Lord of your life. You can trust Him with everything.

Do your friends know Jesus? What would you say if someone asked you about Him? Today's verse says you should always be ready with an answer when someone asks about Jesus.

Don't be shy. Be ready to share with others what you know. Then Jesus can be the Lord of their lives too.

Dear Jesus, I want to share You with everyone. Please show me how.

1 Peter 3:15 CEV

Honor Christ and let him be the
Lord of your life. Always be ready
to give an answer when someone
asks you about your hope.

33

....

Jesus Helps Me to Be Strong

Imagine going ice-skating for the first time. Your feet hit the ice, and off you go. But then you fall. At first, you feel sad that you fell. But then you remember that God is with you and is helping you, and that makes you so very happy! So you get up and try again. This time you go a little farther before you fall. You feel like giving up, but you ask Jesus to help you keep trying. Soon you are skating! Your heart fills with joy because Jesus was with you while you did something hard. Trusting Him brought you joy!

Jesus gives you strength to keep on trying. In hard times when you feel like giving up, remember the joy you have because Jesus is with you, helping you to be strong and brave.

Jesus, I feel joyful knowing that You are with me.

Nehemiah 8:10 ICB

The joy of the Lord will
make you strong.

34

Goodnight and Sleep Well!

In the Bible, King David told about his faith in God. He said that even if thousands of his enemies surrounded him, he could lie down and sleep peacefully. King David could fall asleep because he trusted God to protect him. He was sure he would wake up in the morning, safe and sound, because God was watching over him.

God watches over you, too, when you sleep. In the dark, quiet night there is nothing to be afraid of. Nighttime is a soft, gentle time when you can lie in bed and feel God all around you. He is there when you fall asleep. He will stay with you all night. When you wake up in the morning, God is still with you, ready to start a brand-new day.

Dear God, I know I will sleep
peacefully tonight because
You are watching over me.

Psalm 3:5-6 ICB

I can lie down and go to sleep.
And I will wake up again because
the Lord protects me. Thousands
of enemies may
surround me. But
I am not afraid.

35

....

I Will Serve the Lord

You know what is right and what is wrong. But maybe you don't always want to do what is right. Maybe you don't want to clean your room, be kind to your brothers and sisters, or come inside when your mom calls you. Maybe you don't want to go to sleep at your bedtime or eat broccoli or do your school assignment when you should. Maybe there are times when you just want to say, "No!"

You face right and wrong choices every day. It is up to you to decide what to do. When you make a right choice, you obey God. It pleases Him. When you choose what is wrong, God is sad, but He is so happy when you ask Him to forgive you and ask for help to do what's right.

Think about right and wrong choices today. Will you do whatever you want, or will you please God by doing what is right?

God, please help me choose
what's right every day.

Joshua 24:15 ICB

You must decide whom you
will serve. . . . As for me and my
family, we will serve the Lord.

36

God's Best Gift

God wants everyone to be saved, so He gave the gift of salvation. If you accept His gift, you'll live with Him in heaven one day. But without God's gift, you can't go to heaven because are all filled up with sin. So how can you accept His gift?

Some people think they can be saved by being good all the time. You show God respect by being good, but doing good things won't save you. You can be saved by believing that Jesus took away your sins when He died on the cross and rose again. If you ask God to forgive your sins and you believe in what Jesus did, then you will be saved and can go to heaven someday.

Salvation isn't something you have to earn. It is God's best gift for you. He loves you and wants you to live with Him forever.

Dear Jesus, thank You for taking away my sins. Your salvation is the very best gift.

Ephesians 2:8-9 CEV

You were saved by faith in God, who treats us much better than we deserve. This is God's gift to you, and not anything you have done on your own. It isn't something you have earned, so there is nothing you can brag about.

37

Fear Not!

In Isaiah 41:10, God says, "Fear not." That means *don't be afraid.* Then God gave us several reasons why we don't have to be scared. He is the one-and-only God, and He is always with you. He promises to make you strong to face whatever problems get in your way. God promises to help you. It will be like He is holding you in His hand, keeping you safe there with Him.

All kids—and grownups too—have things they are afraid of: the dark, spiders, roller coasters, bees, or something else frightening. Being afraid is part of being human. So the next time you feel afraid, you can remember God's promises. He is always with you. He will make you strong. Fear not!

Dear God, when I feel afraid, I will remember Your promises. I know You are with me and will help me.

Isaiah 41:10 NKJV

"Fear not, for I am with you; be not dismayed, for I am your God. I will strengthen you, yes, I will help you, I will uphold you with My righteous right hand."

38

....

Good Thoughts

Close your eyes. Be very quiet and listen. Now name all the sounds you hear.

The world is a noisy place. Many of the things we hear stick in our brains: songs, words people say, or stuff we hear on TV. All of those things can get in the way of hearing God's voice in our hearts. That's why God wants us to think good thoughts that bring us closer to Him.

Begin each day by thinking about God. Pray. Read the Bible or recite Bible verses you memorized. Get in the habit of talking with God all day. If your mind becomes so filled with other things that you can't think about God, go someplace quiet. Spend a few minutes alone with your heavenly Father. Ask Him to fill your head with good thoughts that remind you of Him.

Heavenly Father, fill up my
head with good thoughts that
bring me closer to You.

Philippians 4:8 NIV

Finally, brothers and sisters,
whatever is true,
whatever is noble,
whatever is right,
whatever is pure,
whatever is lovely,
whatever is admirable—
if anything is excellent
or praiseworthy—think
about such things.

39

God Is My Shield

The front window in a car is called a windshield. A shield is something that protects you. A windshield protects you from the wind; otherwise everything in the car would be blowing around. A shield is a good thing to have.

The Bible says that God is a shield. He protects you. God helps you to be strong when you need to decide between right and wrong. He makes you strong when you are afraid to try something new. You can always trust God to help you.

God is the only One with superpowers. And think about it: He chose *you* to love and protect! What a happy promise from God! So show God how happy you are. Make up a thank-you song and sing it to Him.

Thank You, God, for being my shield! You protect me and make me strong.

Psalm 28:7–8 NCV

The LORD is my strength and shield. I trust him, and he helps me. I am very happy, and I praise him with my song. The LORD is powerful; he gives victory to his chosen one.

40

I Am God's Helper

God uses people of all ages to help do His work here on earth. And He loves using kids to be His helpers! You can help Him by being a good example for other kids to follow. Let your words always be respectful. Be kind, gentle, and caring. Look for kids who are lonely or not well-liked, and be their friend. Be loving and forgiving. And remember to tell other kids about Jesus.

Kids can do God's work in many ways. They can make cards for children in the hospital, pick up trash to help keep the earth clean, make cookies and share them with a neighbor, or give something they own to someone in need. Can you think of other ways to help?

Dear God, I want to be Your helper.
Please show me what I can do.

1 Timothy 4:12 ICB

You are young, but do not let anyone treat you as if you were not important. Be an example to show the believers how they should live. Show them with your words, with the way you live, with your love, with your faith, and with your pure life.

41

A Place in Heaven

After He died on the cross and came alive again, Jesus had news for His friends. He told them He was going back to heaven to be with His Father, God. That made His friends sad. They loved Jesus! They would miss Him.

Jesus told them not to be sad. He was going to set up rooms for them in heaven. The friends wouldn't go there just yet. It would be a long time. But when they got there, Jesus would have new rooms waiting for them.

Jesus has a room in heaven for you too. It's the best room ever! But you'll have to wait to see it. While you wait here on earth, you can spend time with Jesus and live a life pleasing to God.

Dear Jesus, thank You for wanting me to live with You in heaven someday.

John 14:2-3 NCV

"There are many rooms in my Father's house; I would not tell you this if it were not true. I am going there to prepare a place for you. After I go and prepare a place for you, I will come back and take you to be with me so that you may be where I am."

42

Blessings!

When God made the sun, He put it the perfect distance from our world. The sun warms the earth and gives us light. It helps plants to grow too.

King David said that God is like the sun. He gives us light by showing us the way to live. He helps us grow strong in our trust in Him. He brightens up our days and makes us happy. God is also like a shield, King David said. He protects us and helps us when we are in trouble.

God wants to take care of us because He loves us so much. God also wants us to love and obey Him, and He is so happy when we thank Him for His blessings, which are all the good things He does for us. God loves to bless us!

Dear God, You brighten my life like sunshine! Thank You for all Your blessings.

Psalm 84:11 NIV

For the LORD God is a sun and shield; the LORD bestows favor and honor; no good thing does he withhold from those whose walk is blameless.

43

Run the Race with Jesus

Imagine trying to run a race through a forest. Trees get in your way. You trip over rocks and sticks. But what if you could get rid of everything in your way?

The Bible says that life is like a race where sin gets in your way. During your life you'll run into all kinds of trouble that you need to get rid of. But don't be afraid; Jesus will help you. Maybe you need to decide between doing what is right or wrong. Ask Jesus to help you decide. Maybe you feel disappointed, sad, or angry. Ask for Jesus' help.

Now imagine running a race in a forest again, except this time Jesus is leading you. He will help you take the right path. That's the kind of friend He is. Jesus goes ahead of you, helping you make right choices so you can live a life pleasing to God.

Thank You, Jesus, for helping me get rid of the sin that gets in my way.

Hebrews 12:1-2 ICB

So we have many people of
faith around us. Their lives tell
us what faith means. So let us
run the race that is before us
and never give up. We should
remove from our lives anything
that would get in the way.
And we should remove the
sin that so easily catches us.
Let us look only to Jesus.

44

....

He Counts My Tears

What makes you cry? Maybe you cried when you got hurt or when someone hurt your feelings. A disagreement with a friend could make you cry. So could missing someone or not getting to do something you really wanted to do. There are many reasons people cry.

God understands all those reasons. He sees your tears. He even counts them! God keeps a list of every tear that falls from your eyes (Psalm 56:8). He writes down how many tears you cry. One . . . two . . . three . . .

God doesn't want you to be sad. Whatever happens, He will work it out for your good. He promises to wipe every tear from your eyes and to comfort you.

God, You must really love me
if You care enough to count
my tears. I love You too!

Revelation 21:4 NIV

He will wipe every tear
from their eyes.

45

Trust Jesus

You can trust Jesus with everything! He is honest all the time and keeps His promises. Jesus is kind and gentle, never mean. He always knows what is going on with you, and He knows exactly what is right for you. Jesus promises to be with you every day, all day—forever!

What does it mean to trust Jesus with all your heart? It means you believe that He is perfect in every way. You never have to worry that Jesus will lead you to do something wrong.

People make bad choices sometimes, but Jesus never does. Whenever you aren't sure what to do, you can put your trust in Him. Trust Jesus with everything you do. Remember that He is with you all the time and ready to help.

Jesus, I trust You with all my heart.

Proverbs 3:5-6 ICB

Trust the Lord with all your heart. Don't depend on your own understanding. Remember the Lord in everything you do. And he will give you success.

46

Patience

You've probably heard the words "Be patient!" more than a few times. When you want something badly, it's hard to wait. Being patient is like looking at a big, wrapped present for a long time. You know it's for you. Something wonderful is inside. But you can't tear off the wrapping paper and open the box just yet. You have to wait.

Patience isn't fun, but it *is* good for you. Patience helps you to trust God's timing. If you think about God while you wait, patience becomes easier. You can remember that God is working on something great for you. It's not done yet. But it's coming at exactly the time God knows you need it.

If you have trouble being patient, ask God to help you. He will teach you to trust Him and wait patiently for everything.

Dear God, I'm not always good at waiting. Please help me be patient.

James 1:4 ICB

Let your patience show itself perfectly in what you do. Then you will be perfect and complete. You will have everything you need.

47

God Gives Me Power

Imagine a situation where you have to make a tough decision. You know the right thing to do, but the right thing to do seems scary. Maybe you feel afraid to talk with a new kid in your class. You know that you could show God's love by being friendly, but you worry, *Will he be friendly back to me? Will he like me?* You should never be afraid to do what is right. God gave you a spirit of courage. Instead of wondering if the new kid will be friendly, you could focus on making him feel welcome. God will take care of the rest.

God gives you power to crush your scared feelings. When you step up and do what you know is right, He replaces them with feelings of love for others. When you put fear away and focus on others, then you help God spread His love around.

God, please give me courage
to put away what makes me
scared and do what is right.

2 Timothy 1:7 ICB

God did not give us a spirit
that makes us afraid. He
gave us a spirit of power
and love and self-control.

48

Tell the World: God Is Great

Look at me. I'm so great!"

"I can do everything better than you."

"Ha, ha! I have more than you!"

Bragging is when we talk about how great we are or how much we have. God is not pleased when people brag. Instead, God wants us to be grateful to Him for His blessings.

There is one kind of bragging that does please God. He loves it when people talk about how great He is. Brag about God all you want! Tell others that you know Him. Remind people that God is kind, loving, and fair. When you're tempted to talk about how great you are, tell others how great God is instead!

Father God, thank You for
reminding me not to brag
unless I'm talking about You.

Jeremiah 9:24 ICB

"If someone wants to brag, let him brag about this: Let him brag that he understands and knows me. Let him brag that I am the Lord. Let him brag that I am kind and fair. Let him brag that I do things that are right on earth. This kind of bragging pleases me," says the Lord.

49

God's Plan for Me

God has a plan for you. He knew what your whole life would be like even before you were born. And God's plan is a great one because He chose you to be like His Son, Jesus.

Jesus was always kind and patient. He didn't wish He had what someone else had. He didn't brag about the great things He did. Jesus was perfect. He trusted His Father, God, with everything.

God's plan is for you to be as much like Jesus as you can. But you will never be perfect, like Jesus. Sometimes you will do sinful things that are not pleasing to God. Still, God will use those times to help you learn to be more like His Son. You can trust God to use everything—even bad things—to bring about something good.

God, thank You for having a plan for me and for helping me be more like Jesus.

Romans 8:28 NCV

We know that in everything God works for the good of those who love him. They are the people he called, because that was his plan.

50

Please Forgive Me

The young shepherd boy, David, grew up to be a great king. But just like everyone else, King David was not perfect. There were times when he messed up. David knew that he could always pray and ask God to forgive him. He wrote today's verse because he was sorry for the wrong things he did, and he could trust God to forgive him.

Like King David, there are times when you mess up and make wrong choices. God will forgive you too, but you need to ask for His forgiveness.

It's easy. Simply tell God what you did wrong. Tell Him that you are sorry, and ask Him to forgive you. He will! God will forgive you every time. And He doesn't keep track of your wrongs. As soon as God forgives you, it is like the wrong thing you did never happened. That's true forgiveness!

Dear God, I'm thankful that
You will always forgive me,
no matter what I've done.

Psalm 51:1-2 CEV

You are kind, God! Please have pity on me. You are always merciful! Please wipe away my sins. Wash me clean from all of my sin and guilt.

51

....

More Like Jesus

One day a fuzzy caterpillar stopped eating. It found a strong twig and began spinning itself a cocoon. Then it rested inside. While it rested, the caterpillar's body began to change. Its shape changed. The caterpillar grew wings and became a butterfly! It broke out of the cocoon and flew around, showing off its brand-new self.

When you believe that Jesus died on the cross for your sins, it is a little like becoming a butterfly. Your body doesn't change, like the caterpillar's did, but you change inside. Your old self is gone, and you become more like Jesus. When you trust in Him, Jesus makes good changes in your life. You become more kind, helpful, and forgiving.

Others will see how you've changed. "What's different?" they might ask.

Then you can say, "Jesus is making me more like Him!"

God, make me more like You.

2 Corinthians 5:17 CEV

Anyone who belongs to Christ
is a new person. The past is
forgotten, and everything is new.

52

......

Powerful Words

As soon as you say a word, you give it power. The words you say can make people feel good about themselves. But some words can be so hurtful that they make people cry. Words can tell the truth or a lie. Some words are so powerful that people never forget them. You are always the one who decides what kind of power to give your words.

Jesus' words were always good and kind. His words were never lies. Everything He said had the power to help people. Jesus always knew just what to say.

Think about your words today. Think about them before you let them leave your mouth. Then do your best to make them powerfully good!

I will think about my words, Father. I want everything I say to be kind and helpful to others.

Colossians 4:6 NCV

When you talk, you should
always be kind and pleasant
so you will be able to answer
everyone in the way you should.

53

Garbage In, Garbage Out

Think about a stinky pail of garbage filled with leftovers like banana peels and potato skins. The longer the garbage stays in the pail, the stinkier it gets until someone empties the garbage. Garbage in. Garbage out.

When you think mean thoughts about people or if you watch something on TV you shouldn't, it is like you are putting garbage into your brain. If you don't get rid of those stinky thoughts, they spill over into your heart. Before long, the garbage comes out of you in bad language and actions.

Be careful with the things you put in your brain. Make sure your thoughts and words are always good and pleasing to God.

Heavenly Father, please help me make wise choices about the thoughts I put in my brain.

Psalm 19:14 ICB

I hope my words and thoughts
please you. Lord, you are my
Rock, the one who saves me.

54

Jesus, I Need . . .

Everyone needs air to breathe, food to eat, and water to drink. We also need a place to live, and we need love from family and friends.

Jesus knows what you need all the time. He knows even before you do if you will need to wear a warm jacket tomorrow or if you need an extra blanket on your bed. He knows if you need a hug or if you need help learning something new. Jesus knows it all! He will always bless you with exactly what you need, exactly when you need it.

Maybe you need something big, like a broken arm healed. Or maybe you need something little, like a friend with an umbrella on a rainy day. Whatever it is, pray and ask Jesus for it. He is always with you and loves to help.

Jesus, I trust You to give
me everything I need.

Philippians 4:19 CEV

I pray that God will take care
of all your needs with the
wonderful blessings that
come from Christ Jesus!

55

Amazing, Wonderful God

Read Isaiah 40:12, and answer the questions. Was your answer "God" for each one?

God looks down from heaven. He sees everything on earth and in the sky. He knows exactly how big and deep the oceans are. Does the sky go on forever? God knows. How much does a mountain weigh? God knows. He even knows how much dust is on earth. God knows because He made it all—the earth, sky, mountains, and oceans. Everything! Best of all, God knows all about you—your name, what you like and dislike, and even how many hairs are on your head. God knows because He made you.

Take time today to look around and notice all the wonderful things God made. You will find plenty. His work is everywhere!

I look around at everything You made, and I see how amazing and wonderful You are.

Isaiah 40:12 ICB

Who has measured the oceans in the palm of his hand? Who has used his hand to measure the sky? Who has used a bowl to measure all the dust of the earth? Who has used scales to weigh the mountains and hills?

56

Put God First

The most important relationship in Jesus' life was with His Father, God. Even when He was a little boy, Jesus made spending time with His Father more important than anything else.

One time Jesus' family was worried that He was lost. While they were on their way home after a festival, they realized Jesus wasn't with them. They searched and searched until they found Jesus in the temple, where people worship and learn about God (Luke 2:41–52). Instead of going home to play, Jesus chose to spend more time with God. He wanted to learn what God wanted Him to do.

God wants you to be like Jesus and put God first. God should be more important to you than anything else. So spend time thinking about Him and talking with Him. And make God the most important part of your life.

Dear God, help me put You first.

Matthew 6:33 ICB

"The thing you should want
most is God's kingdom and
doing what God wants. Then
all these other things you
need will be given to you."

57

Fill Up with Joy

The world is filled with joyful things. Playgrounds to play in. Zoos to visit. Family fun. Friends. Parties at church and at school. The list of happy things goes on and on!

What makes you happy? Are you happy all the time?

Are you happy when you and your best friend don't get along? Are you joyful when you look forward to something and then find out it isn't going to happen? Of course not!

Everyone has times when they feel unhappy. But even in those unhappy times, there is one good reason to feel joyful—God! Even on your worst days, He gives you plenty of reasons to be happy.

The next time you feel unhappy, try this: play "I Spy God." Look around for all the good things God does.

God, help me see the good things You've put all around me.

Philippians 4:4 ICB

Be full of joy in the Lord always. I will say again, be full of joy.

58

Two Houses

Jesus told a story about two men. Each was building a house. One man listened to God and obeyed Him. He built his house on a rock. The other man did not listen to God. He did what he thought was best. He built his house on sand.

A big storm came. Rain poured down. Rivers flooded. Wind beat against both houses. The house on the rock stood strong. But the other house built on the sand fell down with a *crash*! If that builder had only listened to God and obeyed Him, his house would have been strong too (Matthew 7:24–27).

Jesus' story has a lesson: "Without the help of the Lord," your plans will not turn out right. Whatever you do, always ask for God's help and obey Him. God knows the best way. Everything He does is right.

In whatever I do, God, I will
remember to ask for Your help.

Psalm 127:1 CEV

Without the help of the LORD it is useless to build a home or to guard a city.

59

....

Follow Jesus

Imagine that someone offered to give you a toy you really wanted. You knew the toy was stolen and that you shouldn't take it. Would you give up what you wanted and say no?

Jesus told His followers, "If anyone wants to follow me, he must say 'no' to the things he wants." Jesus meant that people should put what God wants ahead of their own wants. God would not want you to take a stolen toy, even if you really, *really* wanted it!

Sometimes it's hard to follow Jesus and do what God wants, especially when God's desires are different from your own. Still, it is always best to choose His way.

Dear Jesus, I want to follow You.
Please help me put what God
wants ahead of what I want.

Mark 8:34 ICB

Then Jesus called the crowd to him, along with his followers. He said, "If anyone wants to follow me, he must say 'no' to the things he wants. He must be willing to die on a cross, and he must follow me."

60

God's Treasure Map

Have you been on a treasure hunt? First, someone hides something special. If that person gives directions to find the treasure, then you can search for it. Without directions, you would never find the treasure. You would be lost.

The Bible is like a treasure map. Everything you should know about God is hidden inside. As you read the Bible and learn what is in there, you come closer to God. You discover how He wants you to live. The more you learn from the Bible, the wiser you become.

Read the Bible each day, or have someone read it to you. Think about what it says. Memorize Bible verses. Then put what you learn to use—obey God's words. When you live to please Him, you will have found the treasure. Your life will be filled with His blessings.

Dear God, help me learn more about You each day.

Joshua 1:8 NCV

"Always remember what is written in the Book of the Teachings. Study it day and night to be sure to obey everything that is written there. If you do this, you will be wise and successful in everything."

61

No One Is Perfect

Jesus always does the right thing. He is perfect. We try to be perfect too, but sometimes we do the wrong thing. Why? Because no one but Jesus is perfect! And because we mess up, we can't be perfect until we get to heaven. Until then, God wants us to do our best to please Him.

You can please God by learning from the Bible. Try to follow God's rules. Set a good example for others. When you mess up and make wrong choices, ask God to forgive you. Then stop worrying about what you did. Move on and do your best not to make those mistakes again.

Think about how Jesus lived. You won't be perfect like He is, but you should do your best to be like Him.

Thank You, God, for helping me to be like You. I will do my best to please You.

Philippians 3:12 ICB

I do not mean that I am already as God wants me to be. I have not yet reached that goal. But I continue trying to reach it and to make it mine. Christ wants me to do that. That is the reason Christ made me his.

62

The Helper

God is your Helper. You can't see God, but His Spirit is all around you. He sees everything. He helps with everything. Whenever there is something you think you can't do, you can trust God to help.

God even helps you pray. Sometimes, praying is easy. The words come just as if you were talking with someone sitting in front of you. Other times praying is hard. You don't know what to say, but you know you should say something. When words don't come, you can ask God to pray for you. He knows the right words.

If your words get stuck, you can say, "God, please help me pray." Then be quiet for a while. You can't hear God praying for you, but know that He is.

Heavenly Father, please help me pray each day.

Romans 8:26 CEV

In certain ways we are weak, but the Spirit is here to help us. For example, when we don't know what to pray for, the Spirit prays for us in ways that cannot be put into words.

63

God Leads the Way!

If you were picked to stand up in church and say a Bible verse, would your tummy feel like it were filled with butterflies? If you were in a play, would you worry that you would forget what you're supposed to do?

Being worried and afraid is part of life. But the Bible teaches us not to be afraid. It reminds us that God goes with us wherever we go—and He stays with us.

God isn't afraid of anything! He goes ahead of you, leading the way. He won't ever forget about you or leave you behind.

The next time you feel worried or afraid, imagine yourself following God, walking in His footsteps. You'll never have to worry, because God is right there keeping you safe.

Lead the way, God! I'm right behind You, and I won't be afraid.

Deuteronomy 31:8 ICB

The Lord himself will go before you. He will be with you. He will not leave you or forget you. Don't be afraid. Don't worry.

64

God Wants My Worries

Everyone worries. Sometimes, the things we care about make us feel restless, nervous, and maybe even afraid. The worries pile up. If we could stuff them all into a suitcase, they wouldn't fit. The lid wouldn't shut, even if we sat on it!

There's a better way to deal with worries. Give them to God! God loves you so much, and He does not want you to have such a heavy heart. When you give your worries to God, your heart will start to feel lighter.

Say this little prayer: "Heavenly Father, please take away all my worries." God promises to take care of you. You can trust Him to care for you every day.

You've got my worries, God. I trust that You know what to do with them.

1 Peter 5:6–7 NIV

Humble yourselves, therefore, under God's mighty hand, that he may lift you up in due time. Cast all your anxiety on him because he cares for you.

65

The Sneaky One

God's enemy is Satan. Satan is the sneaky one who wants you to make wrong choices. He is called a thief because he tries to steal away God's best for you. He tries to trick God's children into messing up. But God is good; He protects His children from what Satan wants.

The Bible will help you keep Satan away by teaching you right from wrong. When Satan tries to lead you to a wrong choice, you will know what God wants. All you have to do is follow God's rules and say no to wrong choices.

If you aren't sure what to do, ask Jesus. Jesus is your best friend and protector. He came to save you from sin. He wants you to have the best life ever. If you stay close to Him, Jesus will help you do what is good and right. Then you won't fall for Satan's sneaky tricks.

Jesus, please lead me always to choose what is right.

John 10:10 NKJV

"The thief does not come except to steal, and to kill, and to destroy. I have come that they may have life, and that they may have it more abundantly."

66

Jesus Always

Fences and walls can keep people apart. So can long distance, when one person lives far from another. But the Bible says that nothing on earth, or anyplace else, can keep us apart from Jesus.

Jesus is always with you. Nothing will ever keep you from Him. You could travel to the moon and back, and Jesus would never leave your side. He goes where you go. When you are sleeping, He watches over you. And He is still there when you wake up in the morning.

Jesus said He will love you always, but His promise is even bigger than that. He promises that nothing will ever separate you from Him! And one day you will be together with Jesus in heaven. Isn't that a wonderful promise?

Thank You, Jesus, for always being with me. I love You!

Romans 8:38–39 ICB

Yes, I am sure that nothing can separate us from the love God has for us. Not death, not life, not angels, not ruling spirits, nothing now, nothing in the future, no powers, nothing above us, nothing below us, or anything else in the whole world will ever be able to separate us from the love of God that is in Christ Jesus our Lord.

67

We're Better Together

The first person God created was a man named Adam. In the beginning, Adam was alone. But God decided that was not good. So God made a friend for Adam. Her name was Eve.

God knows it isn't good for you to be alone either. He wants other people in your life: family members, friends to play with, teachers, and especially people to help you know God.

It's important to meet friends and teachers who know God, because together you learn to be God's helpers. Being with other people who believe in God helps you learn the ways God wants you to love and forgive others.

In the Bible, a follower of Jesus named Paul said that it is important to be with others who love God. When people who love God get together, their love for God grows even stronger.

Dear God, thank You for
friends who know You.

Hebrews 10:24-25 ICB

Let us think about each other and help each other to show love and do good deeds. You should not stay away from the church meetings, as some are doing. But you should meet together and encourage each other. Do this even more as you see the Day coming.

68

The King's Statue

The Bible says King Nebuchadnezzar had a big gold statue. The king commanded everyone to bow down and worship his statue. The king's helper told the people, "When you hear the music from the king's band, you must worship the statue. If you don't, you will be thrown into the fiery furnace!"

Three men named Shadrach, Meshach, and Abednego loved God. They would only bow to God and would not bow to the king's statue. They believed if they were put in the king's furnace, God would protect them. But no matter what, they would not bow to the statue. So the king had them thrown into the fire. But they were not burned because God was with them.

Remember this—whatever happens, God is right there with you, just as He was with Shadrach, Meshach, and Abednego.

God, whatever happens,
I will trust You.

Daniel 3:17-18 ICB

You can throw us into the blazing furnace. The God we serve is able to save us from the furnace and your power. If he does this, it is good. But even if God does not save us, we want you, our king, to know this: We will not serve your gods. We will not worship the gold statue you have set up.

69

Working for Jesus

Hard work is, well, hard! Some work is so hard that you want to give up. You wonder why you need to put so much effort into getting something done.

Jesus doesn't want you to quit. Instead, He wants you to work hard for Him. He wants you to remember that every good thing you do, every project you finish, is for Him.

When you work hard, Jesus sees, and He is pleased with your work. Others see your hard work too. That sets a good example, and Jesus loves it when you show others how to follow Him.

If you feel like giving up, keep going! Keep working hard for Jesus, and don't allow anything to get in your way.

> Dear Jesus, I want to do good work for you and for others. Please help me never give up.

1 Corinthians 15:58 NIV

Therefore, my dear brothers and sisters, stand firm. Let nothing move you. Always give yourselves fully to the work of the Lord, because you know that your labor in the Lord is not in vain.

70

God Protects Me

Baby chicks are so cute! Yellow and fluffy, they tumble around their mother hen, staying close to her warm body. Hens are good mothers. They protect their chicks. If danger is nearby, the mother hen spreads her wings over her babies to protect them. There, the baby chicks are safe.

God protects you even better than a mother hen protects her chicks. When you need protection, God covers you with His blanket of love and strength. You can't see it, but believe that it's there. You are God's child, and His love for you is wonderful.

Whenever you feel worried or afraid, talk to God. He hears you. He loves you and will always protect you.

Father God, I feel safe knowing that You watch over and protect me.

Psalm 17:7-8 ICB

Your love is wonderful. By
your power you save from
their enemies those who
trust you. Protect me as you
would protect your own eye.
Protect me as a bird hides
her young under her wings.

71

Share the Good News

The Bible tells us about Paul, one of Jesus' followers. Paul loved God with all his heart. He understood that Jesus was God's greatest gift to us. It was Jesus, God's Son, who took away our sins and gave us a way to heaven. Paul wanted everyone to believe in what Jesus did. He wanted everyone to go to heaven someday and live with God. So Paul traveled everywhere telling people about Jesus.

Paul knew that some people hated him for talking about Jesus. But Paul didn't care. The most important thing to him was spreading the good news about Jesus. He let nothing get in his way.

You can be like Paul and spread the good news too. Tell your friends about Jesus. Remind them that those who believe in Jesus will go to heaven someday.

God, I want to share the good news like Paul did. Please show me how.

Acts 20:24 NCV

I don't care about my own life.
The most important thing is
that I complete my mission,
the work that the Lord Jesus
gave me—to tell people the
Good News about God's grace.

72

In Jesus' Name

When you pray, you are talking with the Creator of the universe, the one true God. Wow! That's more amazing than talking with presidents or kings or anyone famous. God is greater than all of them. And He loves talking with you.

Did you know that God likes it when you use Jesus' name in your prayers? It shows that you trust in all the great things Jesus does. When you pray, you can simply end your prayers by saying, "In Jesus' name, amen."

When you pray, don't be afraid to ask God for what you want. But remember, He knows what you need. If you don't get what you want, it may be that God has something even better in His plans for you.

Father God, I love that I can talk with You. Please help me be more like You. In Jesus' name, I pray, amen.

John 16:23 NKJV

"In that day you will ask Me nothing. Most assuredly, I say to you, whatever you ask the Father in My name He will give you."

73

....

When I Don't Want To

I don't want to clean my room today."

"I don't want to go to school."

"I don't want to leave the playground yet."

Everyone has things they don't want to do. You can complain about them, or you can find a way to make those times easier.

Jesus is always with you. So He is with you even when you have to do things you don't want to do. Imagine Jesus being with you when you clean your room, go to school, or walk away from the playground. It's hard to do things you don't want to do, but Jesus helps you and reminds you that obeying with a good attitude makes God happy.

Practice remembering that Jesus is with you. Then, no matter what you have to do, try your best to have a good attitude as a way to honor God.

Jesus, help me to have a good attitude all day.

Colossians 3:23 NKJV

Whatever you do, do it heartily, as to the Lord and not to men.

74

Everything Comes from God

Newborn babies come with nothing. In that first minute of a baby's life, he or she doesn't even have clothes. Babies have a mom, a dad, and maybe older brothers and sisters. That's all!

But right away, babies get stuff: clothes, toys, books, and warm, cuddly blankets. As the babies get older and become young children, they get more stuff: maybe an action-hero toothbrush, a sparkly headband, or a backpack for school.

God makes sure that everyone has everything they need. And sometimes, when He knows it's best, God takes things away. Still, we should praise God for everything. Without God, we would have nothing. And no matter what, He will always take care of us.

God, thank You for making me and for all Your wonderful gifts.

Job 1:21 CEV

We bring nothing at birth; we take nothing with us at death. The LORD alone gives and takes. Praise the name of the LORD!

75

....

How Much Does It Cost?

Imagine having some money in your pocket. Would you exchange your money for some ice cream, or would you rather have a new toy?

Things cost money.

But how much does it cost to buy God's blessings? Nothing! You don't have to buy blessings or do anything to earn them. God does wonderful, kind things for you each day. He wants to give you good things because He loves you so much.

You can thank God for His blessings by doing your best to live right and by making good choices. If you mess up, God will give you His *grace*—that means He will forgive you. He will continue to bless you because You are His amazing, wonderful, and much-loved child.

Heavenly Father, thank You
for Your blessings, and thank
You for Your grace.

Titus 2:11 ICB

That is the way we should live, because God's grace has come. That grace can save every person.

76

Shine Your Light

What do you do when it gets dark? You turn on lights in your house so you can see what you are doing.

Matthew 5:14–15 says that you can be like a light God shines on the world. God wants you to tell others about Him. When you tell others, you help brighten the world with God's love. God wants your light to be so bright that it is like a city with big, shining lights on a hilltop! Then whenever people hear you speak about God, they will be reminded of His love.

Don't hide your light. Let it shine! Tell others the good news that God sent His Son, Jesus, to save the world. And because He did, everyone has a way to heaven.

> Dear God, I will tell others
> about You. I will help light
> the world with Your love.

Matthew 5:14-15 ICB

"You are the light that gives light to the world. A city that is built on a hill cannot be hidden. And people don't hide a light under a bowl. They put the light on a lampstand. Then the light shines for all the people in the house."

77

I'm Satisfied

When you visit a toy store, you see many toys that you want. But as much as you would like to have them, it's important to remember that you can't get them all. You can't have everything you want all the time.

God asks you to be satisfied with what you have. To be satisfied means that you are okay with having only what God gives you and nothing more. He gives you everything you need. That, all by itself, should make you satisfied. But God gives you more than just what you need—He gives you best friends, games to play, laughter, and even some of the toys you want. His blessings are everywhere!

Practice being satisfied with only what you need. Then, when you get something you want, it will be even more special.

> God, thank You for giving me everything I need and some of the things I want.

Philippians 4:11 NCV

I have learned to be satisfied with the things I have and with everything that happens.

....

78

A Child of God

Did you know that your parents have authority over you? They give you what you need to live a good life. Your parents give you shelter and food to eat and also give you rules to obey.

Have your parents ever told you to brush your teeth before bed? You probably obeyed, even if you didn't feel like it! Being obedient is important because your parents know how to take care of you, and their rules help you live in the best way.

If you decide to follow God, then God becomes your parent too. God will provide for your needs and teach you how to live. God also promises to give you His Spirit, and His Spirit reminds us to do what's right.

God is a wonderful and caring Father. You can trust Him to always keep His promises and to take care of you.

Father God, I love being
one of Your children.

Galatians 4:6–7 CEV

Now that we are his children, God has sent the Spirit of his Son into our hearts. And his Spirit tells us that God is our Father. . . . You are God's children, and you will be given what he has promised.

159

79

A Quick Look at Heaven

God allowed His friend, John, a quick look into heaven. John wrote about it in the Bible.

John saw God sitting on His throne. An amazing green rainbow circled around God, and God Himself glowed brightly like beautiful jewels. People dressed in white robes and gold crowns gathered around Him. They bowed before God. They sang songs of praise to Him. Four strange creatures—they looked like a lion, an ox, a man, and a flying eagle—sang their own song of worship: "Holy, holy, holy, is the Lord God All-Powerful. He was, he is, and he is coming" (Revelation 4:8 ICB). Everything in heaven praised God.

That is what God wants us to do here on earth too—praise Him. He is greater than anyone or anything, and He deserves our praise.

God, You alone are great
and mighty. I honor and
praise You every day.

Revelation 4:11 NIV

You are worthy, our Lord and God, to receive glory and honor and power, for you created all things, and by your will they were created and have their being.

80

God Lives in My Heart

How well do you take care of your body? Do you eat healthy food? Do you exercise? How about washing your hands and brushing your teeth? There are many good reasons to take care of your body. But the most important reason is God!

God's Spirit lives inside your heart. His Spirit is invisible; you can't see it. It doesn't take up space inside you. But God's Spirit is in there. His Holy Spirit is the part of God that guides you, teaches you to live right, and blesses you with everything you need.

You can keep your heart a clean place for God's Spirit by making right choices and worshipping Him. God wants us to take care of our bodies—both the inside and out!

Dear God, I want my heart to be a clean place for You. I will do my best to obey You and do what is right.

1 Corinthians 6:19 ICB

You should know that your body is a temple for the Holy Spirit. The Holy Spirit is in you. You have received the Holy Spirit from God. You do not own yourselves.

81

....

A Checkup with God

When you go to the doctor for a checkup, he or she listens to your heart. The doctor looks into your throat and eyes and then checks your body to make sure everything is working right.

God gives you checkups sometimes too. His checkups are different. Instead of a body checkup, God looks inside your heart and knows everything about you. He checks your thoughts to see if they are good. God also checks the words you say.

If something doesn't check out, God will remind you of it. You might feel a little guilty about a wrong choice you made or something you said. But don't worry! Tell God about it, and ask Him to forgive you. He will wipe away anything bad that He found and mark "perfect" on your checkup.

Check me out, God. Examine
me. If you find anything
wrong, forgive me please.

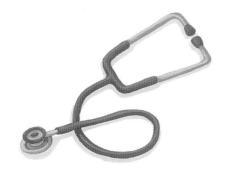

Psalm 139:23-24 ICB

God, examine me and know my heart. Test me and know my thoughts. See if there is any bad thing in me. Lead me in the way you set long ago.

82

God Knows Everything!

Why can't I see God? How can He be everywhere at the same time? Why do bad things happen? And why doesn't God heal all the sick people?

Everyone has questions about God. There are some things about Him that we just won't know. God is much smarter than any person is or ever will be—He knows everything! His thoughts are greater than anything we could ever understand. But the way God does things is always perfect and true.

When you have questions about God and there are no answers, just trust that He knows what He is doing. You might not always agree with God's decisions. But you can count on this: He never makes mistakes. God always does what is good and right.

God, I know I won't understand
everything about You. Help me trust
You even when I can't understand.

Isaiah 55:8–9 NIV

"For my thoughts are not your thoughts, neither are your ways my ways," declares the LORD. "As the heavens are higher than the earth, so are my ways higher than your ways and my thoughts than your thoughts."

83

God's Great, Great Love

What is the biggest thing you have ever seen? Mountains are high. Oceans are wide and deep. The sky goes on and on beyond anything a human can see. All of these things are big.

Jesus' friend, Paul, wanted everyone to know that God's love is bigger and greater than anything on earth. He wanted people to understand that God's love is bigger than the biggest mountain. His love is deeper than the deepest ocean. God's love never ends.

Do you believe that God loves you with His big, wide, and deep love? He fills you with His great love forever.

Say a prayer right now, and ask God to fill up your family and friends with His love.

God, please fill up my family and friends with Your great big, forever love.

Ephesians 3:18-19 ICB

I pray that you and all God's
holy people will have the power
to understand the greatness
of Christ's love. I pray that you
can understand how wide and
how long and how high and how
deep that love is. Christ's love
is greater than any person can
ever know. But I pray that you
will be able to know that love.
Then you can be filled with the
fullness of God.

84

Give It Up

Sacrifice means to give up something you want for someone else. You might sacrifice the last brownie so your sister can have it. Or you could sacrifice a fun playdate to attend your aunt's birthday party.

Jesus made the greatest sacrifice of all. He gave up His life so people could live forever with God in heaven. Dying on the cross wasn't an easy thing to do. But Jesus did it anyway because He loves God and us so much.

God wants you to make a sacrifice for Him too. He wants you to give up wrong choices and live in a way that pleases Him. Each day, choose to obey and honor God, even if it isn't easy. That is the best way to show God how much you love Him.

Heavenly Father, I want to give up what's wrong and do what is right. Will You help me, please?

Romans 12:1 CEV

Dear friends, God is good. So I beg you to offer your bodies to him as a living sacrifice, pure and pleasing. That's the most sensible way to serve God.

85

A Father's Wise Advice

King David loved God. But there were times in his life when David made wrong choices. The older he became, the more David learned about pleasing God.

One day God decided it was time for David to give up his job as king. The new king would be David's son Solomon. But before David gave up his job to his son, he shared some wise advice.

King David told Solomon to worship God only and obey Him. He reminded Solomon that God would always watch over him. God would know if Solomon made right or wrong choices. And David told Solomon to stay near to God and pray. Otherwise, God would seem far away.

David's advice is good for you too. Remember to worship and obey God. Do your best, every day, to stay close to God and please Him.

Teach me, God, to live right and please You.

I Chronicles 28:9 CEV

Solomon, my son, worship God
and obey him with all your heart
and mind, just as I have done.
He knows all your thoughts and
your reasons for doing things,
and so if you turn to him, he will
hear your prayers.

86

God's Never-ending Love

"Get up! Get up! It's a brand-new day!"

When you get up in the morning, you don't know what wonderful surprises God has waiting for you. He loves you, so keep your eyes and ears open. His little gifts are all around you. Maybe there will be pancakes for breakfast this morning. A colorful butterfly might land on your shoulder. You could meet a new friend. At bedtime, there will be hugs and cuddles and maybe a story or two.

God's love is all around you. It never ends. He is always ready to give you everything you need and more! Thank God when you get up in the morning and before you go to sleep at night. Thank Him because He is good!

God, You are so good to me.
Thank you for this day!

Lamentations 3:22–23 ICB

The Lord's love never ends.
His mercies never stop. They
are new every morning. Lord,
your loyalty is great.

87

The Golden Rule

If someone says something mean to you, do you say something mean back? If a friend is selfish about sharing toys, are you selfish about sharing your toys too? What if someone makes a face at you? Do you make a mean face back?

Jesus gave His followers a rule. Some people call it the golden rule. It says, "In everything, do to others what you would have them do to you."

Even when people are selfish and unkind, you should respond with kindness. If someone says something mean, you should answer with something nice. If a friend won't share his toys, you should still share yours. If someone makes a face, don't make a mean face back.

When you treat people the way you want to be treated, it makes the world a happier place—and that makes God happy!

Jesus, I like Your golden rule. I will do my best to obey it every day.

Matthew 7:12 NIV

"So in everything, do to others
what you would have them
do to you, for this sums up
the Law and the Prophets."

88

God's Book About Me

God knew you before you were born. He made you. He gave you a body and He made it grow. He gave you a brain that thinks and a heart that loves. Even before you were born, God knew about every day of your life.

And here is something really special—God has a book in heaven all about you! The Bible says that God wrote in your book before you were even born. He wrote about everything you would do every day of your life.

God is never surprised by anything that happens to you. It is all written down ahead of time. He knows what will happen and how He will help you. You will never have to worry. God always has everything in your life under control. He understands you, and He loves you.

God, thank You for loving me and knowing everything about me! I feel safe knowing You are with me.

Psalm 139:16 CEV

With your own eyes you saw my
body being formed. Even before
I was born, you had written in
your book everything I would do.

89

God's Not Done Yet

Maybe you started working a puzzle but got bored with it. Or maybe you started coloring a page, and before you finished, you decided to color another page instead. Maybe you put away just a few of your toys.

Everyone leaves some things undone. But God, the great Creator, isn't like that. He finishes everything He starts, every time. He works at everything until it is perfect.

God began working on you even before you were born. He will work on you every day of your life to make you the best you can be. Each day you will learn something new about life and about Him. God will not be done working on you until you meet Him in heaven one day. Then you will be His perfectly finished creation forever.

Keep working on me, God. Make me the best that I can be.

Philippians 1:6 NCV

God began doing a good work in you, and I am sure he will continue it until it is finished when Jesus Christ comes again.

90

Troubles

Jesus had troubles when He lived on earth. Jesus had done nothing wrong, but soldiers arrested Him anyway. They hit Him and even spit on Him. They put Jesus on a cross to die. Jesus allowed all these troubles to happen to Him so that we could be saved and live in heaven with Him someday. That is a blessing that will last forever!

Jesus' troubles may seem really big compared to yours. But whatever you are troubled with—no matter how big or small—God will take care of you. He will never leave you to face trouble alone. You can't see God, but believe that He is with you. And remember that your problems won't last forever. If you believe in Jesus, one day all your troubles will be gone and you will live happily in heaven.

Thank You, God, for always staying close and taking care of me.

2 Corinthians 4:17–18 NCV

We have small troubles for a while now, but they are helping us gain an eternal glory that is much greater than the troubles. We set our eyes not on what we see but on what we cannot see. What we see will last only a short time, but what we cannot see will last forever.

91

What Is Faith?

I hope everything I read in the Bible is true."

"I hope Jesus loves me."

"I hope God forgives me when I say, 'I'm sorry.'"

Hoping is a lot like wishing: you wish for something, but you aren't sure if your wish will come true.

Everything about the Bible, God, and Jesus is true. If you believe that, then you have faith. *Faith* means knowing for sure—even if you can't see it—that something is real. When you have faith, you are able to say things like this:

"I know everything I read in the Bible is true."

"I know Jesus loves me."

"I know God forgives me when I say, 'I'm sorry.'"

When you believe that everything about the Bible, God, and Jesus is real and true, then your faith will grow big and strong.

God, I have faith! I believe that everything I know about You is true.

Hebrews 11:1 ICB

Faith means being sure of the things we hope for. And faith means knowing that something is real even if we do not see it.

92

Sleepy Time

You had a long, busy day. It was so much fun, but now you are tired. You need big, strong arms to pick you up and carry you to bed.

Jesus understands those long, busy days. He had plenty of them here on earth. Jesus often had big crowds of people around Him, wanting to hear Him teach about God. But sometimes Jesus had to leave the crowds so He could go someplace and rest.

When you're tired, you need to get away from it all and rest. When you've had a hard day, go to Jesus and tell Him about it. He will take your worries away and will give you rest in His big, strong arms.

Jesus lives in heaven now, and He never sleeps or needs to rest. He promises to watch over you all night long. So, little one, sleep well tonight in Jesus' care. Sweet dreams!

Good night, Jesus. Thank You for helping me rest. I love You.

Matthew 11:28 NKJV

....

"Come to Me, all you who
labor and are heavy laden,
and I will give you rest."

93

....

What Is Temptation?

Temptation is something that pulls you toward doing what you know is wrong. Maybe your parents said, "No cookies before dinner." But the cookies look so good. Should you take one—or not?

Satan loves temptation. He loves pulling you toward making wrong choices.

Satan tried to trick Jesus into making wrong choices too. But Jesus knew how to escape temptation. He trusted God to help. When Satan tried to trick Jesus into doing something wrong, Jesus answered Satan with what God says is right. And after a while, Satan gave up.

Keep your eyes open for Satan's tricks. When temptation pulls you toward doing something wrong, say, "No!" Say it as often as you have to until the temptation goes away.

Dear God, please help me
say no to temptation.

1 Corinthians 10:13 ICB

The only temptations that you have are the temptations that all people have. But you can trust God. He will not let you be tempted more than you can stand. But when you are tempted, God will also give you a way to escape that temptation. Then you will be able to stand it.

94

A Tiny Mustard Seed

A mustard seed is very, very tiny. But if you plant that little seed, it will grow into a big bush. This small seed has the power to make something huge happen!

Jesus compared a mustard seed to faith in God. Jesus said that even a little bit of faith can make something great happen. You don't have to be afraid to face anything. When you trust in God, nothing will be too big to get in your way, not even a mountain.

Faith in God—even a tiny amount—will make big things happen. So put your faith in God today, and see what amazing things will happen.

Father God, with You, nothing is impossible. Help me put my faith in You, no matter what mountains I face.

Matthew 17:20 icb

"If your faith is as big as a mustard seed, you can say to this mountain, 'Move from here to there.' And the mountain will move. All things will be possible for you."

95

Praise God!

Look at the stars on a clear night. They go on forever. They remind us of God, the Creator. Sunrises, snow-covered mountain tops, oceans, and shooting stars—so many things remind us of how wonderful and powerful our God is. When we see them, we think, *Wow! God, how did You do that?*

The Bible tells us to praise God for His greatness. After all, He created everything, and He's the only One who can give us a fresh start and fill us with joy forever. God is so worthy of praise! You can praise God by telling Him you think He is awesome. You can praise Him by singing songs about how great He is. You can dance, clap your hands, and say, "Thank You, God, for all You do!"

God sees you, loves you, and cares for you. Aren't those great reasons to praise Him?

I praise You, God! You are so
worthy and so wonderful!

Jude vv. 24–25 CEV

Offer praise to God our Savior because of our Lord Jesus Christ! Only God can keep you from falling and make you pure and joyful in his glorious presence. Before time began and now and forevermore, God is worthy of glory, honor, power, and authority. Amen.

96

When I Grow Up

What do you want to be when you grow up? What things would you like to do? You may not know yet what you will be or do when you grow up. But God knows! He has your future all planned out. God already knows if you will get married. He knows if you will have kids and how many. Will you be a teacher or own a store or become a doctor? Will you climb mountains or fly through space to Mars? God knows.

God promises that His plans for you are good. He has so many fun and exciting times waiting for you. When life is hard and not very fun, remember that God has good things waiting for you. So hang on to the things you hope for. Maybe they will happen. Or maybe God has something even better planned. You just have to wait and see.

Father, I believe that You have great plans for me. I'm excited to know what they are.

Jeremiah 29:11 ICB

"I say this because I know what I have planned for you," says the Lord. "I have good plans for you. I don't plan to hurt you. I plan to give you hope and a good future."

97

The Israelites' Song

God's people, the Israelites, sang Psalm 121 while they walked to a city called Jerusalem. The city was high on a hill, and the climb was hard. So while they walked, the people sang about God. They remembered that He is up in heaven, high above the hills. They sang about what a great protector He is.

When you feel as though something is too hard and you want to give up, remember the Israelites' song. You might get tired and need rest, but God never rests. He will protect you and lead you until you get the hard things done.

You can write a song for God too! Your song can tell God why you love Him. And you don't have to wait until you're climbing a mountain to sing it. God always wants to hear your songs.

God, when something seems
too hard, I will sing about
how great You are.

Psalm 121:1–4, 7 ICB

I look up to the hills. But where
does my help come from? My help
comes from the Lord. He made
heaven and earth. He will not let
you be defeated. He who guards
you never sleeps. He who guards
Israel never rests or sleeps. . . .
The Lord will guard you from all
dangers. He will guard your life.

98

......

Yes, I Can!

Jesus' friend, Paul, had trouble. Everywhere he went, he told people about Jesus, and then unpleasant things happened. Paul was in a shipwreck. People beat him and chased him out of their towns. They put Paul in prison because he talked about Jesus. Sometimes he was hungry, thirsty, and cold. But through it all, Jesus helped him. Paul never lost faith in Jesus. He kept traveling, telling people about Jesus wherever he went.

You might not face the same troubles Paul had, but you will have some days when things don't go well. Don't worry! Jesus will help you.

Paul said, "I can do all things through Christ who strengthens me." You can get through your troubles too. Stay close to Jesus. He will give you strength to keep going until those not-so-good days are over.

Jesus, help me trust You everyday,
even on not-so-good days.

Philippians 4:13 NKJV

I can do all things through
Christ who strengthens me.

99

The Lord's Prayer

Matthew 6:9–13 is the Lord's Prayer, a prayer Jesus taught His friends.

The first part reminds us that God is the Father of us all. His name should be respected. We should pray that everyone lives the way God wants them to.

The next part of the Lord's Prayer is the asking part. We should ask God for what we need. We need God to forgive our wrong choices and to help us forgive people who are mean to us or hurt our feelings. Then we should ask God to help us make good choices and to protect us from Satan's temptations.

Have you ever felt unsure about how to pray? The Lord's Prayer can help you. If you're stuck on what to say, use this prayer as a guide. Just remember to honor God with your words and to ask Him for everything you need.

Dear Jesus, thank You for teaching me Your prayer.

Matthew 6:9–13 NKJV

"Our Father in heaven, hallowed be Your name. Your kingdom come. Your will be done on earth as it is in heaven. Give us this day our daily bread. And forgive us our debts, as we forgive our debtors. And do not lead us into temptation, but deliver us from the evil one."

100

Thank You, God!

When your team wins, you clap and shout, "Hip, hip, hooray! Yay! Good job!" You shout because you want the team to know how much you appreciate them.

God enjoys hearing a good shout of appreciation too. He loves it when people praise Him by clapping their hands, playing music, or singing. God also loves hearing sounds in nature. A bird's song or a wolf's howl might sound like a shout of praise to the Lord. A big crash of thunder might be the clouds shouting praises to God! Everything on earth sends up shouts of praise to thank God for the great things He does.

So, come on. Join in with the rest of creation. Shout to the Lord, "Thank You, God!"

Thank You, dear Lord, for being my God. I want to praise You with shouts of joy: You are amazing! I love You, God!

Psalm 100:1-2 ICB

Shout to the Lord, all the earth.
Serve the Lord with joy. Come
before him with singing.

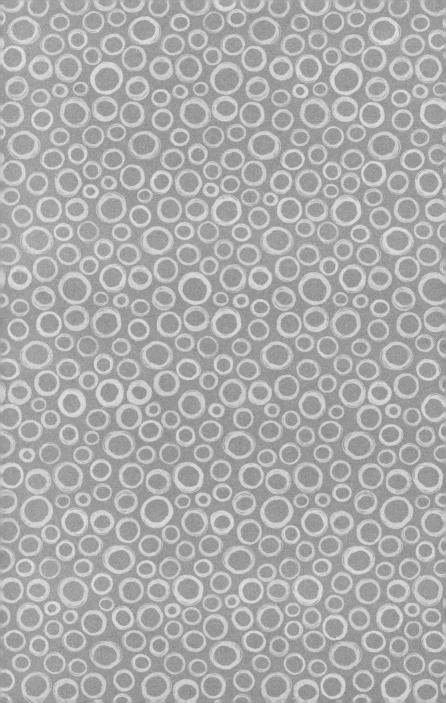